BELOVED

This is YOUR year to create. Make it an AMAZING year, using your intuition and your Tarot cards as a guide.

COPYRIGHT © 2026 BRIGIT ESSELMONT, BIDDY TAROT

ALL RIGHTS RESERVED. THIS BOOK OR ANY PORTION THEREOF MAY NOT BE REPRODUCED OR USED IN ANY MANNER WHATSOEVER WITHOUT THE EXPRESS WRITTEN PERMISSION OF THE AUTHOR EXCEPT FOR THE USE OF BRIEF QUOTATIONS IN A BOOK REVIEW.

PRINTED IN THE UNITED STATES OF AMERICA

WELCOME

You're about to dive into a magical journey to deepen your connection with Tarot and create your most aligned, purposeful year yet!

This Planner is your go-to space for dreaming big, reflecting deeply, and tuning into your intuition.

Here's what's waiting for you inside:

- Tap into the monthly energy with monthly card pulls

- Explore the blessings of each New and Full Moon

- Intentionally create the life you desire with daily Tarot card pulls

- Connect with what each season has in store for you with seasonal Tarot spreads

With your Planner by your side this year, you'll strengthen your inner voice, bring your dreams to life, and stay connected to your Higher Self—all with the wisdom of Tarot guiding you.

So grab a Tarot deck, and let's start weaving your dream year into reality 💜

Much Love,

Brigit xox

P.S.

We love seeing your Planner in action! Share your Planner photos and videos on Instagram with **#biddytarotplanner**, and don't forget to follow **@biddytarot** for more tips to help you stay aligned and inspired all year long.

P.P.S.

Need a Tarot deck to use with your Planner? The Biddy Tarot Deck is a great place to start! It's modern, approachable, and perfect for readers of all levels. You can grab yours here: https://www.biddytarot.com/deck/

FREE BONUS [VALUE $197]
BIDDY TAROT PLANNER TOOLKIT

To make sure you get the absolute most out of your Planner, I've created an exclusive **FREE Bonus Planner Toolkit**—packed with powerful tools and resources to deepen your practice.

Here's what's waiting for you:

- **Step-by-Step Video Tutorials** – Practical guidance to help you use your Planner with ease, including tips for working with Tarot spreads, setting intentions, and staying aligned with your goals.

- **Lunar Magic Meditations** – Harness the energy of the Full Moon and New Moon with guided meditations to keep you in flow.

- **Printable Tarot Cards** – Enjoy printable cards from the Biddy Tarot Deck. Use them as Tarot cards in your practice or print them as stickers to personalize your Planner.

- **Tarot Spreads for Self-Discovery** – Explore my favorite spreads to connect with your intuition and uncover powerful insights.

- **Mercury Retrograde Guide** – Navigate retrograde periods with confidence using practical tips and a custom Tarot spread.

- **Daily Tarot Card Guide** – Build a meaningful daily practice with step-by-step guidance for using the Planner's Daily Tarot Card feature.

And so much more!

DOWNLOAD THE FREE PLANNER TOOLKIT AT
WWW.BIDDYTAROT.COM/FREE-PLANNER-TOOLKIT

TABLE OF CONTENTS

HOW TO MAKE THE MOST OUT OF YOUR PLANNER	1
YEARLY REFLECTION	5
NEW YEAR'S RITUAL	10
NEW YEAR'S TAROT SPREAD	14
JANUARY	19
FEBRUARY	26
MARCH	33
APRIL	40
MAY	47
JUNE	54
JULY	61
AUGUST	68
SEPTEMBER	75
OCTOBER	82
NOVEMBER	89
DECEMBER	96
YEARLY REFLECTION	103
SEASONAL SPREADS	108
LUNAR SPREADS	117
LEARN TO READ TAROT INTUITIVELY	142

HOW TO MAKE THE MOST OUT OF YOUR PLANNER

This Planner is designed to grow with you—no matter when you begin. It's intentionally evergreen, meaning you can start using it at any point in the year and revisit it again and again. Whether you're beginning a new calendar year, celebrating your birthday, or simply entering a new chapter of life, this Planner will help you connect with your intuition, align your energy, and manifest your desires in every season.

Think of it as a living, breathing companion for your personal growth.

Start whenever you feel called. You can begin your journey today—just open to the New Year's Ritual (or your own "New Beginning" ritual) and set powerful intentions for the cycle ahead.

Move through the months at your own rhythm. Each monthly section helps you tune into the energy of the moment, with space for Tarot pulls, intentions, and reflections.

Work with the seasons and lunar cycles. Use the Seasonal and Lunar Spreads to deepen your connection to nature's rhythms, no matter where you are in your personal journey.

Close each cycle intentionally. When you reach a natural transition—year's end, birthday, or major life shift—use the Yearly Reflection to integrate what you've learned and prepare for what's next.

There's no "right" time or way to use this Planner—only the one that feels aligned for you. Let your intuition guide you, return to it often, and allow each page to become a sacred mirror of your growth

To get started, here's what you will need:

- Your favorite Tarot deck (we highly recommend the Biddy Tarot Deck available at www.biddytarot.com/deck)
- Your favorite markers, pens, and pencils
- Your free Bonus Planner Toolkit (download it at biddytarot.com/free-planner-toolkit)

If you're on Social Media, use the hashtag **#biddytarotplanner** to post photos and videos of your Planner and Tarot spreads, and we'll share them with the Biddy Tarot community!

AT THE START OF THE YEAR

Kick things off with the **New Year Ritual**—a simple but powerful practice of self-reflection, journaling, and Tarot. It's your chance to:

- Tap into the energy of the year ahead
- Get clear on your dreams and goals
- Set yourself up for a year that feels aligned and full of possibility

FOR EACH SEASON

Every few months, take a moment to pause and check in with the **Seasonal Tarot Spreads**. These spreads are a great way to:

- Explore the unique energy of each season.
- Set clear intentions for the months ahead.

EACH MONTH

Each month, connect with your Tarot cards to reveal the energy you're calling in.

- **Create a sacred space.** Begin each month with intention. Light a candle, take a few deep breaths, and center yourself in the present moment. Allow this to become your sacred ritual for stepping into the energy of the month ahead.
- **Pull a Tarot card.** Ask your deck, "What energy am I calling in this month?" Draw one card—perhaps just from the Major Arcana if you want to focus on the deeper themes of your journey. Reflect on the card's message. What opportunities are unfolding? What challenges may arise? What energy is calling to be expressed?
- **Set your intentions.** From your insights, decide what you wish to experience, create, or transform this month. Write it down clearly, then translate your intentions into aligned actions—the practical, inspired steps that will bring your vision to life.
- **Track the signs.** As you move through the month, stay present to the synchronicities, lessons, and shifts that mirror your card's energy. Notice how your intentions are manifesting and how your awareness is deepening.
- Reflect at month's end. Return to your Planner and your card. Explore what you've learned, how you've grown, and what this month's energy has revealed. Each month becomes a powerful cycle of intuition, alignment, and transformation.

EACH DAY

Start and end your day with intention:

- **Morning:** Pull a Tarot card to set the tone for your day. Jot down your thoughts and intentions in the Planner.
- **Evening:** Take a moment to reflect—what energy showed up today, and what did your card teach you?

Need a little inspiration for your daily card draw? Check out this guide: https://www.biddytarot.com/daily-tarot-card/

ON THE NEW AND FULL MOONS

The moon's phases are powerful guides for reflecting, letting go, and setting powerful intentions. Here's how to work with each one:

- **New Moon:** Focus on fresh starts, new projects, and personal growth. Set intentions for what you want to call in.
- **Full Moon:** Celebrate your wins, release what's no longer serving you, and cleanse your energy and space.

Then, use your Planner to tap into the lunar energy even more:

- **Try the Lunar Spread:** Use the New or Full Moon spread toward the end of the planner, tailored to the zodiac sign the moon is in.
- **Listen to the Meditation:** Tune in with the New and Full Moon meditations to deepen your connection. (Download them here: biddytarot.com/free-planner-toolkit)

DURING MERCURY RETROGRADE

While it's known for shaking up communication, travel, and tech, Mercury Retrograde is also a great opportunity to:

- Reflect on what you've learned from past experiences.
- Revisit those projects you've been meaning to finish.
- Reassess your priorities and make sure you're on the right track.
- Rework your plans to bring in more clarity and focus.

To help you navigate it all, grab your Mercury Retrograde Survival Guide here: biddytarot.com/free-planner-toolkit

AT THE END OF THE YEAR

Wrap up your year with the **Yearly Reflection** and give yourself a moment to:

- Celebrate everything you've accomplished.
- Reflect on the lessons you've learned along the way.
- Let go of anything that's no longer helping you grow.

Most importantly, don't forget to celebrate yourself. Take a deep breath and recognize just how far you've come!

AND LASTLY, REMEMBER…

To make the most out of this Planner, check out my free video tutorials and bonuses at **biddytarot.com/free-planner-toolkit**

Post photos of your Planner and Tarot spreads to Instagram with the hashtag **#biddytarotplanner**. We'd love to see your Planner in action!

NEED HELP WITH THE CARD MEANINGS?

To make the most out of the Biddy Tarot Planner, all you need is a basic knowledge of the Tarot cards—your intuition will take care of the rest!

However, I know you may also want a little extra guidance along the way. If so, I have two helpful resources for you.

BOOK
THE ULTIMATE GUIDE TO TAROT CARD MEANINGS

In this modern guide to the Tarot card meanings, you'll discover how to interpret the cards in your Tarot readings with ease. An Amazon best-seller, *The Ultimate Guide to Tarot Card Meanings* includes:

- Detailed descriptions of the 78 Tarot cards, including upright and reversed meanings
- What each card means in relationship, work, finance, spiritual, and well-being readings.

This is a must-have reference guide for all Tarot readers, from beginners to professionals, to help you quickly and easily decipher the meaning of your Tarot readings. Buy the book at www.biddytarot.com/guide.

ONLINE COURSE
MASTER THE TAROT CARD MEANINGS

My program, Master the Tarot Card Meanings, is the #1 online Tarot training course to help you instantly and intuitively interpret the 78 cards in the Tarot deck — without memorization.

In Master the Tarot Card Meanings, I'll show you how to build a unique personal connection with the Tarot, using simple yet powerful techniques for interpreting the cards.

Plus, you'll learn the "must-know" systems within the Tarot to make learning the card meanings super simple.

Together, we'll walk through all 78 Tarot cards, so you can master each and every one of them once and for all!

Learn more at www.biddytarot.com/mtcm or start with our free training at www.biddytarot.com/webinar-mtcm

YEARLY REFLECTION

A thoughtful end-of-year ritual and Tarot spread to help you reflect on the past year's experiences and uncover meaningful insights.

YEARLY REFLECTION

At the end of the year, take some time to reflect on the past 12 months and prepare yourself for the year to come.

For each question, journal your intuitive thoughts first. Then, if you feel called to do so, draw a Tarot card to help you go deeper.

1. What were my biggest achievements this past year?
2. What were my biggest challenges this past year?
3. How have I developed as a person?
4. What did I learn this year?
5. How would I describe the past year in just three words?
6. What aspects of this year can I leave behind?
7. What aspects of this year can I bring with me into the next?
8. What new seeds and opportunities are being planted?

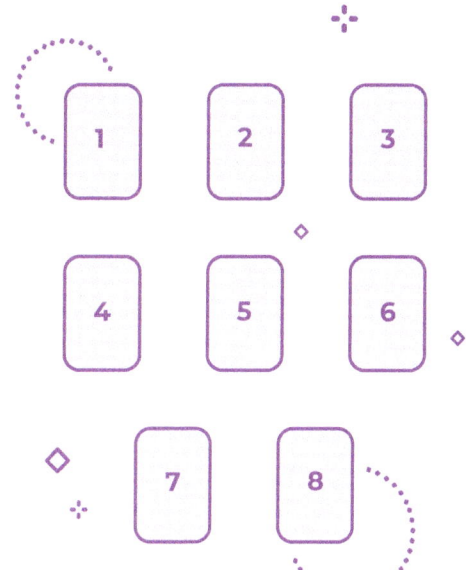

1. WHAT WERE MY BIGGEST ACHIEVEMENTS THIS PAST YEAR?

Don't forget to snap a pic of your reading and share on IG using the hashtag **#biddytarotplanner**. We love seeing you using your Biddy Tarot Planner in action and can't wait to celebrate with you!

2. WHAT WERE MY BIGGEST CHALLENGES FOR THE PAST YEAR?

3. HOW HAVE I DEVELOPED AS A PERSON?

4. WHAT DID I LEARN THIS YEAR?

5. HOW WOULD I DESCRIBE THE PAST YEAR IN JUST THREE WORDS?

6. WHAT ASPECTS OF THIS PAST YEAR CAN I LEAVE BEHIND?

7. WHAT ASPECTS OF THIS PAST YEAR CAN I BRING WITH ME INTO THE NEW YEAR?

8. WHAT NEW SEEDS AND OPPORTUNITIES ARE BEING PLANTED?

NEW YEAR'S RITUAL

This New Year's Ritual is a beautiful, empowering way to start the new year! You'll be connecting with your Higher Self and envisioning what you truly want to manifest in the year to come. This is about positive change and transformation at a deep, symbolic level that will help you to create an abundant, super-charged year ahead.

I encourage you to use this ritual as a guide only. Rituals become even more powerful when you create them, so use this as a starting point and then get creative with what you want to include.

Ready? Let's do it!

STEP 1: CREATE YOUR SACRED SPACE

Gather everything you need for the ritual and begin to create your sacred space.

Next, set up your altar. Your altar doesn't have to be super fancy. Simply use items that represent what you want to manifest in the coming year. You can include crystals, Tarot cards, jewelry, flowers, rocks—whatever helps you to create a sacred intention for your ritual. Place the candles in and around your altar.

When you're all set up and ready, switch off the lights, and light the candles.

Take a moment to ground yourself. Close your eyes and take in a few deep breaths. Connect in with the Earth energy and the Universal energy, feeling yourself filled with a beautiful white light.

STEP 2: REFLECT ON THE PAST YEAR

Reflect on the past year. What did you experience? What were the highs? What were the lows? And what did you learn along the way?

To support you in this process, use the New Year's Tarot Spread on page 14. Draw the first 2 cards and write your insights in the spaces provided.

Then, write your thoughts about the past year on the next page.

BEFORE YOU START, YOU WILL NEED...

- Your Biddy Tarot Planner
- Your favorite Tarot deck—the Biddy Tarot Deck is a great place to start (available via www.biddytarot.com/deck)
- Your favorite markers, pens, or pencils
- At least one candle and some matches
- An herbal bundle for clearing and cleansing
- Items for your altar. These are symbols of what you want to create in the coming year, such as an image of your ideal relationship, a flower for beauty, a seed pod for starting something new—you choose!
- At least one hour of uninterrupted time —lock the door, turn off your phone, do whatever you need to protect your sacred space
- (Optional) Your favorite crystals—I recommend citrine for abundance and clear quartz for clarity
- The New Year's Tarot Spread (on page 14)

Remember, if you would like extra guidance for the New Year's Ritual, watch the free video tutorials at **biddytarot.com/free-planner-toolkit**

INSIGHTS

Take the herbal bundle and light it. Then, wave the smoke around your body, front and back, as you cleanse your aura and release any old energy that may be clinging to you. For each item on your list, say aloud, "I release myself of... {insert what you want to release}."

When you feel complete, say aloud three times, **"I give thanks for the past year. I release what no longer serves me. And I welcome new opportunities with open arms."**

STEP 3: VISUALIZE WHAT YOU WANT TO CREATE IN THE NEW YEAR

Now, close your eyes and start to imagine what you want to create in the year ahead.

Think about what you want to create in your relationships. Imagine it as if it were a movie in your mind, experiencing everything you want to experience in your relationships for the coming year. See yourself being an active participant in the movie.

See what you see. Hear what you hear. Feel what you feel. Taste what you taste. And smell what you smell. Create a full sensory experience.

When you're ready, wipe the movie screen clean, and bring up a new movie, this time about your career, work, and finances. What do you want to create in your material world? Create a full sensory experience.

When you're complete, bring up the next movie for your health and well-being. And after that, your personal development. What do you want to create?

When you feel complete, open your eyes, and write down your experiences on the next page.

Next, take out your Tarot cards and continue with Cards 3 to 9 of the New Year's Tarot Spread. Write your cards and insights in the space provided.

RELATIONSHIPS

HEALTH AND WELL-BEING

CAREER AND FINANCES

PERSONAL DEVELOPMENT

STEP 4: MANIFEST YOUR GOALS FOR THE NEW YEAR

Read over your insights from Step 3 and choose 10 things you want to manifest in the year ahead (e.g. I want to be fit and healthy, or I want to take a 3-month vacation).

Then, change these to "I am" statements (yes, even if they sound a little funny). For example, "I AM fit and healthy" or "I AM enjoying a 3-month vacation." Take a moment to feel the energy and the vibration of these "I am" statements — super powerful, right?!

Now, complete your New Year Tarot Spread from Cards 10 to 12 and write your cards and insights in the spaces provided.

Finally, close your eyes and visualize the energy of what you want to create as a bright white light. Imagine it as a ball of light radiating within your solar plexus (just above your belly button). Then imagine the ball of light getting bigger and bigger, filling your body, flowing through your aura, and illuminating out into the world. This is your power, your determination, your ability to manifest your goals, just as you see them. And so it is done. When you are ready, gently open your eyes.

STEP 5: CLOSE THE SPACE

Before you close the space, check in with your Higher Self and ask if there is anything else that needs to be done before this ritual is complete. Sometimes your intuition may guide you towards another sacred activity before you know for sure that you are done.

When you're ready, say a prayer of thanks to your Higher Self for guiding you along this process. Then, say out loud, "And so it is."

Blow out the candles, turn on the lights, then pack up the space. You may wish to leave part of your altar there or move it somewhere more convenient, so you have a visual reminder of this beautiful ritual that you have gifted yourself.

INSIGHTS

NEW YEAR'S TAROT SPREAD

Gain the clarity you need for your best year yet with the New Year's Tarot Spread. This is a powerful spread to use at the start of the year. Or, you can even use it on your birthday to gain valuable insight into what you might experience during your next year of life.

1. The previous year in summary
2. Lessons learned from the past year
3. Aspirations for the next 12 months
4. What empowers you in reaching your aspirations
5. What may stand in the way of reaching your aspirations
6. Your relationships and emotions in the coming year
7. Your career, work, and finances
8. Your health and well-being
9. Your spiritual energy and inner fulfillment
10. What you most need to focus on in the year ahead
11. Your most important lesson for the coming year
12. Overall, where you are headed in the next 12 months

1. THE PREVIOUS YEAR IN SUMMARY

Excited about what the new year might bring you? Post a pic of your spread using the hashtag #biddytarotplanner and we'll share with the Biddy Tarot community!

2. LESSONS LEARNED FROM THE PAST YEAR

3. ASPIRATIONS FOR THE NEXT 12 MONTHS

4. WHAT EMPOWERS YOU IN REACHING YOUR ASPIRATIONS

5. WHAT MAY STAND IN THE WAY OF REACHING YOUR ASPIRATIONS

6. YOUR RELATIONSHIPS AND EMOTIONS IN THE COMING YEAR

7. YOUR CAREER, WORK, AND FINANCES

8. YOUR HEALTH AND WELL-BEING

9. YOUR SPIRITUAL ENERGY AND INNER FULFILLMENT

10. WHAT YOU MOST NEED TO FOCUS ON IN THE YEAR AHEAD

11. YOUR MOST IMPORTANT LESSON FOR THE COMING YEAR

12. OVERALL, WHERE YOU ARE HEADED IN THE NEXT 12 MONTHS

JANUARY

Monthly Ritual

Start this month by pulling a Tarot card and asking, "What energy am I calling in this month?" Reflect on its message—the opportunities, challenges, and lessons it reveals.

As you look at your calendar below, note any key dates, intentions, or aligned actions connected to your card's energy. Keep the card nearby as a reminder of your focus and inspiration throughout the month.

CARD OF THE MONTH:

HIGHLIGHTS

SUN	MON	TUE	WED	THU	FRI	SAT

Monthly Tarot Card (January)

TAROT CARD:

ENERGY & THEMES FOR THE MONTH
What energy is this card inviting you to embody? What opportunities or challenges might arise?

INTENTIONS & ALIGNED ACTIONS
What do you want to create, experience, or shift this month?Translate your insights into clear intentions and aligned actions.

SIGNS & SYNCHRONICITIES
As the month unfolds, note any patterns, symbols, or moments that mirror your card's message.

END-OF-MONTH REFLECTION
Return to your card and reflect: What unfolded? What did you learn? How did this card support your growth?

JAN 01
▷ INTENTION   CARD OF THE DAY:
▷ REFLECTION

JAN 02
▷ INTENTION   CARD OF THE DAY:
▷ REFLECTION

JAN 03
▷ INTENTION   CARD OF THE DAY:
▷ REFLECTION

JAN 04
▷ INTENTION   CARD OF THE DAY:
▷ REFLECTION

JAN 05
▷ INTENTION   CARD OF THE DAY:
▷ REFLECTION

JAN 06
▷ INTENTION   CARD OF THE DAY:
▷ REFLECTION

JAN 07
▷ INTENTION   CARD OF THE DAY:
▷ REFLECTION

JAN 08
▷ INTENTION   CARD OF THE DAY:
                   ▷ REFLECTION

JAN 09
▷ INTENTION   CARD OF THE DAY:
                   ▷ REFLECTION

JAN 10
▷ INTENTION   CARD OF THE DAY:
                   ▷ REFLECTION

JAN 11
▷ INTENTION   CARD OF THE DAY:
                   ▷ REFLECTION

JAN 12
▷ INTENTION   CARD OF THE DAY:
                   ▷ REFLECTION

JAN 13
▷ INTENTION   CARD OF THE DAY:
                   ▷ REFLECTION

JAN 14
▷ INTENTION   CARD OF THE DAY:
                   ▷ REFLECTION

JAN 15
▷ INTENTION   ▷ REFLECTION

CARD OF THE DAY:

JAN 16
▷ INTENTION   ▷ REFLECTION

CARD OF THE DAY:

JAN 17
▷ INTENTION   ▷ REFLECTION

CARD OF THE DAY:

JAN 18
▷ INTENTION   ▷ REFLECTION

CARD OF THE DAY:

JAN 19
▷ INTENTION   ▷ REFLECTION

CARD OF THE DAY:

JAN 20
▷ INTENTION   ▷ REFLECTION

CARD OF THE DAY:

JAN 21
▷ INTENTION   ▷ REFLECTION

CARD OF THE DAY:

JAN 22
CARD OF THE DAY:
▷ INTENTION
▷ REFLECTION

JAN 23
CARD OF THE DAY:
▷ INTENTION
▷ REFLECTION

JAN 24
CARD OF THE DAY:
▷ INTENTION
▷ REFLECTION

JAN 25
CARD OF THE DAY:
▷ INTENTION
▷ REFLECTION

JAN 26
CARD OF THE DAY:
▷ INTENTION
▷ REFLECTION

JAN 27
CARD OF THE DAY:
▷ INTENTION
▷ REFLECTION

JAN 28
CARD OF THE DAY:
▷ INTENTION
▷ REFLECTION

JAN 29
CARD OF THE DAY:
▷ INTENTION
▷ REFLECTION

JAN 30
CARD OF THE DAY:
▷ INTENTION
▷ REFLECTION

JAN 31
CARD OF THE DAY:
▷ INTENTION
▷ REFLECTION

END OF MONTH INSIGHTS

FEBRUARY

Monthly Ritual

Start this month by pulling a Tarot card and asking, "What energy am I calling in this month?" Reflect on its message—the opportunities, challenges, and lessons it reveals.

As you look at your calendar below, note any key dates, intentions, or aligned actions connected to your card's energy. Keep the card nearby as a reminder of your focus and inspiration throughout the month.

CARD OF THE MONTH:

HIGHLIGHTS:

SUN	MON	TUE	WED	THU	FRI	SAT

Monthly Tarot Card (February)

TAROT CARD:

ENERGY & THEMES FOR THE MONTH
What energy is this card inviting you to embody? What opportunities or challenges might arise?

INTENTIONS & ALIGNED ACTIONS
What do you want to create, experience, or shift this month? Translate your insights into clear intentions and aligned actions.

SIGNS & SYNCHRONICITIES
As the month unfolds, note any patterns, symbols, or moments that mirror your card's message.

END-OF-MONTH REFLECTION
Return to your card and reflect: What unfolded? What did you learn? How did this card support your growth?

FEB 01
CARD OF THE DAY:
▷ INTENTION
▷ REFLECTION

FEB 02
CARD OF THE DAY:
▷ INTENTION
▷ REFLECTION

FEB 03
CARD OF THE DAY:
▷ INTENTION
▷ REFLECTION

FEB 04
CARD OF THE DAY:
▷ INTENTION
▷ REFLECTION

FEB 05
CARD OF THE DAY:
▷ INTENTION
▷ REFLECTION

FEB 06
CARD OF THE DAY:
▷ INTENTION
▷ REFLECTION

FEB 07
CARD OF THE DAY:
▷ INTENTION
▷ REFLECTION

FEB 08
▷ INTENTION ▷ REFLECTION

CARD OF THE DAY:

FEB 09
▷ INTENTION ▷ REFLECTION

CARD OF THE DAY:

FEB 10
▷ INTENTION ▷ REFLECTION

CARD OF THE DAY:

FEB 11
▷ INTENTION ▷ REFLECTION

CARD OF THE DAY:

FEB 12
▷ INTENTION ▷ REFLECTION

CARD OF THE DAY:

FEB 13
▷ INTENTION ▷ REFLECTION

CARD OF THE DAY:

FEB 14
▷ INTENTION ▷ REFLECTION

CARD OF THE DAY:

FEB 15
CARD OF THE DAY:
▷ INTENTION
▷ REFLECTION

FEB 16
CARD OF THE DAY:
▷ INTENTION
▷ REFLECTION

FEB 17
CARD OF THE DAY:
▷ INTENTION
▷ REFLECTION

FEB 18
CARD OF THE DAY:
▷ INTENTION
▷ REFLECTION

FEB 19
CARD OF THE DAY:
▷ INTENTION
▷ REFLECTION

FEB 20
CARD OF THE DAY:
▷ INTENTION
▷ REFLECTION

FEB 21
CARD OF THE DAY:
▷ INTENTION
▷ REFLECTION

FEB 22
CARD OF THE DAY:
▷ INTENTION ▷ REFLECTION

FEB 23
CARD OF THE DAY:
▷ INTENTION ▷ REFLECTION

FEB 24
CARD OF THE DAY:
▷ INTENTION ▷ REFLECTION

FEB 25
CARD OF THE DAY:
▷ INTENTION ▷ REFLECTION

FEB 26
CARD OF THE DAY:
▷ INTENTION ▷ REFLECTION

FEB 27
CARD OF THE DAY:
▷ INTENTION ▷ REFLECTION

FEB 28
CARD OF THE DAY:
▷ INTENTION ▷ REFLECTION

FEB 29

CARD OF THE DAY:

▷ INTENTION

▷ REFLECTION

END OF MONTH INSIGHTS

MARCH

Monthly Ritual

Start this month by pulling a Tarot card and asking, "What energy am I calling in this month?" Reflect on its message—the opportunities, challenges, and lessons it reveals.

As you look at your calendar below, note any key dates, intentions, or aligned actions connected to your card's energy. Keep the card nearby as a reminder of your focus and inspiration throughout the month.

CARD OF THE MONTH:

HIGHLIGHTS:

SUN	MON	TUE	WED	THU	FRI	SAT

Monthly Tarot Card (March)

TAROT CARD:

ENERGY & THEMES FOR THE MONTH
What energy is this card inviting you to embody? What opportunities or challenges might arise?

INTENTIONS & ALIGNED ACTIONS
What do you want to create, experience, or shift this month? Translate your insights into clear intentions and aligned actions.

SIGNS & SYNCHRONICITIES
As the month unfolds, note any patterns, symbols, or moments that mirror your card's message.

END-OF-MONTH REFLECTION
Return to your card and reflect: What unfolded? What did you learn? How did this card support your growth?

MAR 01
CARD OF THE DAY:
▷ INTENTION
▷ REFLECTION

MAR 02
CARD OF THE DAY:
▷ INTENTION
▷ REFLECTION

MAR 03
CARD OF THE DAY:
▷ INTENTION
▷ REFLECTION

MAR 04
CARD OF THE DAY:
▷ INTENTION
▷ REFLECTION

MAR 05
CARD OF THE DAY:
▷ INTENTION
▷ REFLECTION

MAR 06
CARD OF THE DAY:
▷ INTENTION
▷ REFLECTION

MAR 07
CARD OF THE DAY:
▷ INTENTION
▷ REFLECTION

MAR 08
CARD OF THE DAY:
▷ INTENTION
▷ REFLECTION

MAR 09
CARD OF THE DAY:
▷ INTENTION
▷ REFLECTION

MAR 10
CARD OF THE DAY:
▷ INTENTION
▷ REFLECTION

MAR 11
CARD OF THE DAY:
▷ INTENTION
▷ REFLECTION

MAR 12
CARD OF THE DAY:
▷ INTENTION
▷ REFLECTION

MAR 13
CARD OF THE DAY:
▷ INTENTION
▷ REFLECTION

MAR 14
CARD OF THE DAY:
▷ INTENTION
▷ REFLECTION

MAR 15
▷ INTENTION   ▷ REFLECTION

CARD OF THE DAY:

MAR 16
▷ INTENTION   ▷ REFLECTION

CARD OF THE DAY:

MAR 17
▷ INTENTION   ▷ REFLECTION

CARD OF THE DAY:

MAR 18
▷ INTENTION   ▷ REFLECTION

CARD OF THE DAY:

MAR 19
▷ INTENTION   ▷ REFLECTION

CARD OF THE DAY:

MAR 20
▷ INTENTION   ▷ REFLECTION

CARD OF THE DAY:

MAR 21
▷ INTENTION   ▷ REFLECTION

CARD OF THE DAY:

MAR 22
▷ INTENTION ▷ REFLECTION CARD OF THE DAY:

MAR 23
▷ INTENTION ▷ REFLECTION CARD OF THE DAY:

MAR 24
▷ INTENTION ▷ REFLECTION CARD OF THE DAY:

MAR 25
▷ INTENTION ▷ REFLECTION CARD OF THE DAY:

MAR 26
▷ INTENTION ▷ REFLECTION CARD OF THE DAY:

MAR 27
▷ INTENTION ▷ REFLECTION CARD OF THE DAY:

MAR 28
▷ INTENTION ▷ REFLECTION CARD OF THE DAY:

MAR 29
CARD OF THE DAY:
▷ INTENTION
▷ REFLECTION

MAR 30
CARD OF THE DAY:
▷ INTENTION
▷ REFLECTION

MAR 31
CARD OF THE DAY:
▷ INTENTION
▷ REFLECTION

END OF MONTH INSIGHTS

APRIL

Monthly Ritual

Start this month by pulling a Tarot card and asking, "What energy am I calling in this month?" Reflect on its message—the opportunities, challenges, and lessons it reveals.

As you look at your calendar below, note any key dates, intentions, or aligned actions connected to your card's energy. Keep the card nearby as a reminder of your focus and inspiration throughout the month.

CARD OF THE MONTH:

HIGHLIGHTS:

SUN	MON	TUE	WED	THU	FRI	SAT

Monthly Tarot Card (April)

TAROT CARD:

ENERGY & THEMES FOR THE MONTH
What energy is this card inviting you to embody? What opportunities or challenges might arise?

INTENTIONS & ALIGNED ACTIONS
What do you want to create, experience, or shift this month? Translate your insights into clear intentions and aligned actions.

SIGNS & SYNCHRONICITIES
As the month unfolds, note any patterns, symbols, or moments that mirror your card's message.

END-OF-MONTH REFLECTION
Return to your card and reflect: What unfolded? What did you learn? How did this card support your growth?

APR 01
CARD OF THE DAY:
▷ INTENTION
▷ REFLECTION

APR 02
CARD OF THE DAY:
▷ INTENTION
▷ REFLECTION

APR 03
CARD OF THE DAY:
▷ INTENTION
▷ REFLECTION

APR 04
CARD OF THE DAY:
▷ INTENTION
▷ REFLECTION

APR 05
CARD OF THE DAY:
▷ INTENTION
▷ REFLECTION

APR 06
CARD OF THE DAY:
▷ INTENTION
▷ REFLECTION

APR 07
CARD OF THE DAY:
▷ INTENTION
▷ REFLECTION

APR 08
▷ INTENTION   ▷ REFLECTION

CARD OF THE DAY:

APR 09
▷ INTENTION   ▷ REFLECTION

CARD OF THE DAY:

APR 10
▷ INTENTION   ▷ REFLECTION

CARD OF THE DAY:

APR 11
▷ INTENTION   ▷ REFLECTION

CARD OF THE DAY:

APR 12
▷ INTENTION   ▷ REFLECTION

CARD OF THE DAY:

APR 13
▷ INTENTION   ▷ REFLECTION

CARD OF THE DAY:

APR 14
▷ INTENTION   ▷ REFLECTION

CARD OF THE DAY:

APR 15
▷ INTENTION ▷ REFLECTION CARD OF THE DAY:

APR 16
▷ INTENTION ▷ REFLECTION CARD OF THE DAY:

APR 17
▷ INTENTION ▷ REFLECTION CARD OF THE DAY:

APR 18
▷ INTENTION ▷ REFLECTION CARD OF THE DAY:

APR 19
▷ INTENTION ▷ REFLECTION CARD OF THE DAY:

APR 20
▷ INTENTION ▷ REFLECTION CARD OF THE DAY:

APR 21
▷ INTENTION ▷ REFLECTION CARD OF THE DAY:

APR 22
▷ INTENTION　　　　　　　　　CARD OF THE DAY:
▷ REFLECTION

APR 23
▷ INTENTION　　　　　　　　　CARD OF THE DAY:
▷ REFLECTION

APR 24
▷ INTENTION　　　　　　　　　CARD OF THE DAY:
▷ REFLECTION

APR 25
▷ INTENTION　　　　　　　　　CARD OF THE DAY:
▷ REFLECTION

APR 26
▷ INTENTION　　　　　　　　　CARD OF THE DAY:
▷ REFLECTION

APR 27
▷ INTENTION　　　　　　　　　CARD OF THE DAY:
▷ REFLECTION

APR 28
▷ INTENTION　　　　　　　　　CARD OF THE DAY:
▷ REFLECTION

APR 29

CARD OF THE DAY:

▷ INTENTION

▷ REFLECTION

APR 30

CARD OF THE DAY:

▷ INTENTION

▷ REFLECTION

END OF MONTH INSIGHTS

MAY

Monthly Ritual

Start this month by pulling a Tarot card and asking, "What energy am I calling in this month?" Reflect on its message—the opportunities, challenges, and lessons it reveals.

As you look at your calendar below, note any key dates, intentions, or aligned actions connected to your card's energy. Keep the card nearby as a reminder of your focus and inspiration throughout the month.

CARD OF THE MONTH:

HIGHLIGHTS:

SUN	MON	TUE	WED	THU	FRI	SAT

Monthly Tarot Card (May)

TAROT CARD:

ENERGY & THEMES FOR THE MONTH
What energy is this card inviting you to embody? What opportunities or challenges might arise?

INTENTIONS & ALIGNED ACTIONS
What do you want to create, experience, or shift this month? Translate your insights into clear intentions and aligned actions.

SIGNS & SYNCHRONICITIES
As the month unfolds, note any patterns, symbols, or moments that mirror your card's message.

END-OF-MONTH REFLECTION
Return to your card and reflect: What unfolded? What did you learn? How did this card support your growth?

MAY 01
▷ INTENTION   CARD OF THE DAY:
▷ REFLECTION

MAY 02
▷ INTENTION   CARD OF THE DAY:
▷ REFLECTION

MAY 03
▷ INTENTION   CARD OF THE DAY:
▷ REFLECTION

MAY 04
▷ INTENTION   CARD OF THE DAY:
▷ REFLECTION

MAY 05
▷ INTENTION   CARD OF THE DAY:
▷ REFLECTION

MAY 06
▷ INTENTION   CARD OF THE DAY:
▷ REFLECTION

MAY 07
▷ INTENTION   CARD OF THE DAY:
▷ REFLECTION

MAY 08
CARD OF THE DAY:
▷ INTENTION
▷ REFLECTION

MAY 09
CARD OF THE DAY:
▷ INTENTION
▷ REFLECTION

MAY 10
CARD OF THE DAY:
▷ INTENTION
▷ REFLECTION

MAY 11
CARD OF THE DAY:
▷ INTENTION
▷ REFLECTION

MAY 12
CARD OF THE DAY:
▷ INTENTION
▷ REFLECTION

MAY 13
CARD OF THE DAY:
▷ INTENTION
▷ REFLECTION

MAY 14
CARD OF THE DAY:
▷ INTENTION
▷ REFLECTION

MAY 15
CARD OF THE DAY:
▷ INTENTION
▷ REFLECTION

MAY 16
CARD OF THE DAY:
▷ INTENTION
▷ REFLECTION

MAY 17
CARD OF THE DAY:
▷ INTENTION
▷ REFLECTION

MAY 18
CARD OF THE DAY:
▷ INTENTION
▷ REFLECTION

MAY 19
CARD OF THE DAY:
▷ INTENTION
▷ REFLECTION

MAY 20
CARD OF THE DAY:
▷ INTENTION
▷ REFLECTION

MAY 21
CARD OF THE DAY:
▷ INTENTION
▷ REFLECTION

MAY 22
CARD OF THE DAY:
▷ INTENTION
▷ REFLECTION

MAY 23
CARD OF THE DAY:
▷ INTENTION
▷ REFLECTION

MAY 24
CARD OF THE DAY:
▷ INTENTION
▷ REFLECTION

MAY 25
CARD OF THE DAY:
▷ INTENTION
▷ REFLECTION

MAY 26
CARD OF THE DAY:
▷ INTENTION
▷ REFLECTION

MAY 27
CARD OF THE DAY:
▷ INTENTION
▷ REFLECTION

MAY 28
CARD OF THE DAY:
▷ INTENTION
▷ REFLECTION

MAY 29
CARD OF THE DAY:
▷ INTENTION
▷ REFLECTION

MAY 30
CARD OF THE DAY:
▷ INTENTION
▷ REFLECTION

MAY 31
CARD OF THE DAY:
▷ INTENTION
▷ REFLECTION

END OF MONTH INSIGHTS

JUNE

Monthly Ritual

Start this month by pulling a Tarot card and asking, "What energy am I calling in this month?" Reflect on its message—the opportunities, challenges, and lessons it reveals.

As you look at your calendar below, note any key dates, intentions, or aligned actions connected to your card's energy. Keep the card nearby as a reminder of your focus and inspiration throughout the month.

CARD OF THE MONTH:

HIGHLIGHTS

SUN	MON	TUE	WED	THU	FRI	SAT

Monthly Tarot Card (June)

TAROT CARD:

ENERGY & THEMES FOR THE MONTH
What energy is this card inviting you to embody? What opportunities or challenges might arise?

INTENTIONS & ALIGNED ACTIONS
What do you want to create, experience, or shift this month? Translate your insights into clear intentions and aligned actions.

SIGNS & SYNCHRONICITIES
As the month unfolds, note any patterns, symbols, or moments that mirror your card's message.

END-OF-MONTH REFLECTION
Return to your card and reflect: What unfolded? What did you learn? How did this card support your growth?

JUN 01
CARD OF THE DAY:
▷ INTENTION
▷ REFLECTION

JUN 02
CARD OF THE DAY:
▷ INTENTION
▷ REFLECTION

JUN 03
CARD OF THE DAY:
▷ INTENTION
▷ REFLECTION

JUN 04
CARD OF THE DAY:
▷ INTENTION
▷ REFLECTION

JUN 05
CARD OF THE DAY:
▷ INTENTION
▷ REFLECTION

JUN 06
CARD OF THE DAY:
▷ INTENTION
▷ REFLECTION

JUN 07
CARD OF THE DAY:
▷ INTENTION
▷ REFLECTION

JUN 08 CARD OF THE DAY:
▷ INTENTION   ▷ REFLECTION

JUN 09 CARD OF THE DAY:
▷ INTENTION   ▷ REFLECTION

JUN 10 CARD OF THE DAY:
▷ INTENTION   ▷ REFLECTION

JUN 11 CARD OF THE DAY:
▷ INTENTION   ▷ REFLECTION

JUN 12 CARD OF THE DAY:
▷ INTENTION   ▷ REFLECTION

JUN 13 CARD OF THE DAY:
▷ INTENTION   ▷ REFLECTION

JUN 14 CARD OF THE DAY:
▷ INTENTION   ▷ REFLECTION

JUN 15
▷ INTENTION   ▷ REFLECTION   CARD OF THE DAY:

JUN 16
▷ INTENTION   ▷ REFLECTION   CARD OF THE DAY:

JUN 17
▷ INTENTION   ▷ REFLECTION   CARD OF THE DAY:

JUN 18
▷ INTENTION   ▷ REFLECTION   CARD OF THE DAY:

JUN 19
▷ INTENTION   ▷ REFLECTION   CARD OF THE DAY:

JUN 20
▷ INTENTION   ▷ REFLECTION   CARD OF THE DAY:

JUN 21
▷ INTENTION   ▷ REFLECTION   CARD OF THE DAY:

JUN 22
CARD OF THE DAY:
▷ INTENTION
▷ REFLECTION

JUN 23
CARD OF THE DAY:
▷ INTENTION
▷ REFLECTION

JUN 24
CARD OF THE DAY:
▷ INTENTION
▷ REFLECTION

JUN 25
CARD OF THE DAY:
▷ INTENTION
▷ REFLECTION

JUN 26
CARD OF THE DAY:
▷ INTENTION
▷ REFLECTION

JUN 27
CARD OF THE DAY:
▷ INTENTION
▷ REFLECTION

JUN 28
CARD OF THE DAY:
▷ INTENTION
▷ REFLECTION

JUN 29

CARD OF THE DAY:

▷ INTENTION

▷ REFLECTION

JUN 30

CARD OF THE DAY:

▷ INTENTION

▷ REFLECTION

END OF MONTH INSIGHTS

JULY

Monthly Ritual

Start this month by pulling a Tarot card and asking, "What energy am I calling in this month?" Reflect on its message—the opportunities, challenges, and lessons it reveals.

As you look at your calendar below, note any key dates, intentions, or aligned actions connected to your card's energy. Keep the card nearby as a reminder of your focus and inspiration throughout the month.

CARD OF THE MONTH:

HIGHLIGHTS

SUN	MON	TUE	WED	THU	FRI	SAT

Monthly Tarot Card (July)

TAROT CARD:

ENERGY & THEMES FOR THE MONTH
What energy is this card inviting you to embody? What opportunities or challenges might arise?

INTENTIONS & ALIGNED ACTIONS
What do you want to create, experience, or shift this month? Translate your insights into clear intentions and aligned actions.

SIGNS & SYNCHRONICITIES
As the month unfolds, note any patterns, symbols, or moments that mirror your card's message.

END-OF-MONTH REFLECTION
Return to your card and reflect: What unfolded? What did you learn? How did this card support your growth?

JUL 01
▷ INTENTION ▷ REFLECTION CARD OF THE DAY:

JUL 02
▷ INTENTION ▷ REFLECTION CARD OF THE DAY:

JUL 03
▷ INTENTION ▷ REFLECTION CARD OF THE DAY:

JUL 04
▷ INTENTION ▷ REFLECTION CARD OF THE DAY:

JUL 05
▷ INTENTION ▷ REFLECTION CARD OF THE DAY:

JUL 06
▷ INTENTION ▷ REFLECTION CARD OF THE DAY:

JUL 07
▷ INTENTION ▷ REFLECTION CARD OF THE DAY:

JUL 08
CARD OF THE DAY:
▷ INTENTION
▷ REFLECTION

JUL 09
CARD OF THE DAY:
▷ INTENTION
▷ REFLECTION

JUL 10
CARD OF THE DAY:
▷ INTENTION
▷ REFLECTION

JUL 11
CARD OF THE DAY:
▷ INTENTION
▷ REFLECTION

JUL 12
CARD OF THE DAY:
▷ INTENTION
▷ REFLECTION

JUL 13
CARD OF THE DAY:
▷ INTENTION
▷ REFLECTION

JUL 14
CARD OF THE DAY:
▷ INTENTION
▷ REFLECTION

JUL 15
▷ INTENTION   ▷ REFLECTION

CARD OF THE DAY:

JUL 16
▷ INTENTION   ▷ REFLECTION

CARD OF THE DAY:

JUL 17
▷ INTENTION   ▷ REFLECTION

CARD OF THE DAY:

JUL 18
▷ INTENTION   ▷ REFLECTION

CARD OF THE DAY:

JUL 19
▷ INTENTION   ▷ REFLECTION

CARD OF THE DAY:

JUL 20
▷ INTENTION   ▷ REFLECTION

CARD OF THE DAY:

JUL 21
▷ INTENTION   ▷ REFLECTION

CARD OF THE DAY:

JUL 22
CARD OF THE DAY:
▷ INTENTION
▷ REFLECTION

JUL 23
CARD OF THE DAY:
▷ INTENTION
▷ REFLECTION

JUL 24
CARD OF THE DAY:
▷ INTENTION
▷ REFLECTION

JUL 25
CARD OF THE DAY:
▷ INTENTION
▷ REFLECTION

JUL 26
CARD OF THE DAY:
▷ INTENTION
▷ REFLECTION

JUL 27
CARD OF THE DAY:
▷ INTENTION
▷ REFLECTION

JUL 28
CARD OF THE DAY:
▷ INTENTION
▷ REFLECTION

JUL 29 CARD OF THE DAY:
▷ INTENTION ▷ REFLECTION

JUL 30 CARD OF THE DAY:
▷ INTENTION ▷ REFLECTION

JUL 31 CARD OF THE DAY:
▷ INTENTION ▷ REFLECTION

END OF MONTH INSIGHTS

AUGUST

Monthly Ritual

Start this month by pulling a Tarot card and asking, "What energy am I calling in this month?" Reflect on its message—the opportunities, challenges, and lessons it reveals.

As you look at your calendar below, note any key dates, intentions, or aligned actions connected to your card's energy. Keep the card nearby as a reminder of your focus and inspiration throughout the month.

CARD OF THE MONTH:

HIGHLIGHTS:

SUN	MON	TUE	WED	THU	FRI	SAT

Monthly Tarot Card (August)

TAROT CARD:

[ ]

ENERGY & THEMES FOR THE MONTH
What energy is this card inviting you to embody? What opportunities or challenges might arise?

[ ]

INTENTIONS & ALIGNED ACTIONS
What do you want to create, experience, or shift this month? Translate your insights into clear intentions and aligned actions.

[ ]

SIGNS & SYNCHRONICITIES
As the month unfolds, note any patterns, symbols, or moments that mirror your card's message.

[ ]

END-OF-MONTH REFLECTION
Return to your card and reflect: What unfolded? What did you learn? How did this card support your growth?

[ ]

AUG 01
CARD OF THE DAY:
▷ INTENTION
▷ REFLECTION

AUG 02
CARD OF THE DAY:
▷ INTENTION
▷ REFLECTION

AUG 03
CARD OF THE DAY:
▷ INTENTION
▷ REFLECTION

AUG 04
CARD OF THE DAY:
▷ INTENTION
▷ REFLECTION

AUG 05
CARD OF THE DAY:
▷ INTENTION
▷ REFLECTION

AUG 06
CARD OF THE DAY:
▷ INTENTION
▷ REFLECTION

AUG 07
CARD OF THE DAY:
▷ INTENTION
▷ REFLECTION

AUG 08
▷ INTENTION   ▷ REFLECTION   CARD OF THE DAY:

AUG 09
▷ INTENTION   ▷ REFLECTION   CARD OF THE DAY:

AUG 10
▷ INTENTION   ▷ REFLECTION   CARD OF THE DAY:

AUG 11
▷ INTENTION   ▷ REFLECTION   CARD OF THE DAY:

AUG 12
▷ INTENTION   ▷ REFLECTION   CARD OF THE DAY:

AUG 13
▷ INTENTION   ▷ REFLECTION   CARD OF THE DAY:

AUG 14
▷ INTENTION   ▷ REFLECTION   CARD OF THE DAY:

AUG 15
▷ INTENTION　　　　　　　CARD OF THE DAY:
▷ REFLECTION

AUG 16
▷ INTENTION　　　　　　　CARD OF THE DAY:
▷ REFLECTION

AUG 17
▷ INTENTION　　　　　　　CARD OF THE DAY:
▷ REFLECTION

AUG 18
▷ INTENTION　　　　　　　CARD OF THE DAY:
▷ REFLECTION

AUG 19
▷ INTENTION　　　　　　　CARD OF THE DAY:
▷ REFLECTION

AUG 20
▷ INTENTION　　　　　　　CARD OF THE DAY:
▷ REFLECTION

AUG 21
▷ INTENTION　　　　　　　CARD OF THE DAY:
▷ REFLECTION

AUG 22
CARD OF THE DAY:
▷ INTENTION
▷ REFLECTION

AUG 23
CARD OF THE DAY:
▷ INTENTION
▷ REFLECTION

AUG 24
CARD OF THE DAY:
▷ INTENTION
▷ REFLECTION

AUG 25
CARD OF THE DAY:
▷ INTENTION
▷ REFLECTION

AUG 26
CARD OF THE DAY:
▷ INTENTION
▷ REFLECTION

AUG 27
CARD OF THE DAY:
▷ INTENTION
▷ REFLECTION

AUG 28
CARD OF THE DAY:
▷ INTENTION
▷ REFLECTION

AUG 29
CARD OF THE DAY:
▷ INTENTION
▷ REFLECTION

AUG 30
CARD OF THE DAY:
▷ INTENTION
▷ REFLECTION

AUG 31
CARD OF THE DAY:
▷ INTENTION
▷ REFLECTION

END OF MONTH INSIGHTS

SEPTEMBER

CARD OF THE MONTH:

HIGHLIGHTS:

Monthly Ritual

Start this month by pulling a Tarot card and asking, "What energy am I calling in this month?" Reflect on its message—the opportunities, challenges, and lessons it reveals.

As you look at your calendar below, note any key dates, intentions, or aligned actions connected to your card's energy. Keep the card nearby as a reminder of your focus and inspiration throughout the month.

SUN	MON	TUE	WED	THU	FRI	SAT

Monthly Tarot Card (September)

TAROT CARD:

ENERGY & THEMES FOR THE MONTH
What energy is this card inviting you to embody? What opportunities or challenges might arise?

INTENTIONS & ALIGNED ACTIONS
What do you want to create, experience, or shift this month? Translate your insights into clear intentions and aligned actions.

SIGNS & SYNCHRONICITIES
As the month unfolds, note any patterns, symbols, or moments that mirror your card's message.

END-OF-MONTH REFLECTION
Return to your card and reflect: What unfolded? What did you learn? How did this card support your growth?

SEP 01
▷ INTENTION　　　　　　　　　　　CARD OF THE DAY:
▷ REFLECTION

SEP 02
▷ INTENTION　　　　　　　　　　　CARD OF THE DAY:
▷ REFLECTION

SEP 03
▷ INTENTION　　　　　　　　　　　CARD OF THE DAY:
▷ REFLECTION

SEP 04
▷ INTENTION　　　　　　　　　　　CARD OF THE DAY:
▷ REFLECTION

SEP 05
▷ INTENTION　　　　　　　　　　　CARD OF THE DAY:
▷ REFLECTION

SEP 06
▷ INTENTION　　　　　　　　　　　CARD OF THE DAY:
▷ REFLECTION

SEP 07
▷ INTENTION　　　　　　　　　　　CARD OF THE DAY:
▷ REFLECTION

SEP 08
CARD OF THE DAY:
▷ INTENTION ▷ REFLECTION

SEP 09
CARD OF THE DAY:
▷ INTENTION ▷ REFLECTION

SEP 10
CARD OF THE DAY:
▷ INTENTION ▷ REFLECTION

SEP 11
CARD OF THE DAY:
▷ INTENTION ▷ REFLECTION

SEP 12
CARD OF THE DAY:
▷ INTENTION ▷ REFLECTION

SEP 13
CARD OF THE DAY:
▷ INTENTION ▷ REFLECTION

SEP 14
CARD OF THE DAY:
▷ INTENTION ▷ REFLECTION

SEP 15
▷ INTENTION　　　　　　　　　　　　CARD OF THE DAY:
▷ REFLECTION

SEP 16
▷ INTENTION　　　　　　　　　　　　CARD OF THE DAY:
▷ REFLECTION

SEP 17
▷ INTENTION　　　　　　　　　　　　CARD OF THE DAY:
▷ REFLECTION

SEP 18
▷ INTENTION　　　　　　　　　　　　CARD OF THE DAY:
▷ REFLECTION

SEP 19
▷ INTENTION　　　　　　　　　　　　CARD OF THE DAY:
▷ REFLECTION

SEP 20
▷ INTENTION　　　　　　　　　　　　CARD OF THE DAY:
▷ REFLECTION

SEP 21
▷ INTENTION　　　　　　　　　　　　CARD OF THE DAY:
▷ REFLECTION

SEP 22
CARD OF THE DAY:
▷ INTENTION
▷ REFLECTION

SEP 23
CARD OF THE DAY:
▷ INTENTION
▷ REFLECTION

SEP 24
CARD OF THE DAY:
▷ INTENTION
▷ REFLECTION

SEP 25
CARD OF THE DAY:
▷ INTENTION
▷ REFLECTION

SEP 26
CARD OF THE DAY:
▷ INTENTION
▷ REFLECTION

SEP 27
CARD OF THE DAY:
▷ INTENTION
▷ REFLECTION

SEP 28
CARD OF THE DAY:
▷ INTENTION
▷ REFLECTION

SEP 29 CARD OF THE DAY:

▷ INTENTION ▷ REFLECTION

SEP 30 CARD OF THE DAY:

▷ INTENTION ▷ REFLECTION

END OF MONTH INSIGHTS

OCTOBER

Monthly Ritual

Start this month by pulling a Tarot card and asking, "What energy am I calling in this month?" Reflect on its message—the opportunities, challenges, and lessons it reveals.

As you look at your calendar below, note any key dates, intentions, or aligned actions connected to your card's energy. Keep the card nearby as a reminder of your focus and inspiration throughout the month.

CARD OF THE MONTH:

HIGHLIGHTS:

SUN	MON	TUE	WED	THU	FRI	SAT

Monthly Tarot Card (October)

TAROT CARD:

ENERGY & THEMES FOR THE MONTH
What energy is this card inviting you to embody? What opportunities or challenges might arise?

INTENTIONS & ALIGNED ACTIONS
What do you want to create, experience, or shift this month? Translate your insights into clear intentions and aligned actions.

SIGNS & SYNCHRONICITIES
As the month unfolds, note any patterns, symbols, or moments that mirror your card's message.

END-OF-MONTH REFLECTION
Return to your card and reflect: What unfolded? What did you learn? How did this card support your growth?

OCT 01
CARD OF THE DAY:
▷ INTENTION
▷ REFLECTION

OCT 02
CARD OF THE DAY:
▷ INTENTION
▷ REFLECTION

OCT 03
CARD OF THE DAY:
▷ INTENTION
▷ REFLECTION

OCT 04
CARD OF THE DAY:
▷ INTENTION
▷ REFLECTION

OCT 05
CARD OF THE DAY:
▷ INTENTION
▷ REFLECTION

OCT 06
CARD OF THE DAY:
▷ INTENTION
▷ REFLECTION

OCT 07
CARD OF THE DAY:
▷ INTENTION
▷ REFLECTION

OCT 08
CARD OF THE DAY:
▷ INTENTION
▷ REFLECTION

OCT 09
CARD OF THE DAY:
▷ INTENTION
▷ REFLECTION

OCT 10
CARD OF THE DAY:
▷ INTENTION
▷ REFLECTION

OCT 11
CARD OF THE DAY:
▷ INTENTION
▷ REFLECTION

OCT 12
CARD OF THE DAY:
▷ INTENTION
▷ REFLECTION

OCT 13
CARD OF THE DAY:
▷ INTENTION
▷ REFLECTION

OCT 14
CARD OF THE DAY:
▷ INTENTION
▷ REFLECTION

OCT 15
CARD OF THE DAY:
▷ INTENTION
▷ REFLECTION

OCT 16
CARD OF THE DAY:
▷ INTENTION
▷ REFLECTION

OCT 17
CARD OF THE DAY:
▷ INTENTION
▷ REFLECTION

OCT 18
CARD OF THE DAY:
▷ INTENTION
▷ REFLECTION

OCT 19
CARD OF THE DAY:
▷ INTENTION
▷ REFLECTION

OCT 20
CARD OF THE DAY:
▷ INTENTION
▷ REFLECTION

OCT 21
CARD OF THE DAY:
▷ INTENTION
▷ REFLECTION

OCT 22
▷ INTENTION   ▷ REFLECTION
CARD OF THE DAY:

OCT 23
▷ INTENTION   ▷ REFLECTION
CARD OF THE DAY:

OCT 24
▷ INTENTION   ▷ REFLECTION
CARD OF THE DAY:

OCT 25
▷ INTENTION   ▷ REFLECTION
CARD OF THE DAY:

OCT 26
▷ INTENTION   ▷ REFLECTION
CARD OF THE DAY:

OCT 27
▷ INTENTION   ▷ REFLECTION
CARD OF THE DAY:

OCT 28
▷ INTENTION   ▷ REFLECTION
CARD OF THE DAY:

OCT 29
CARD OF THE DAY:
▷ INTENTION
▷ REFLECTION

OCT 30
CARD OF THE DAY:
▷ INTENTION
▷ REFLECTION

OCT 31
CARD OF THE DAY:
▷ INTENTION
▷ REFLECTION

END OF MONTH INSIGHTS

NOVEMBER

Monthly Ritual

Start this month by pulling a Tarot card and asking, "What energy am I calling in this month?" Reflect on its message—the opportunities, challenges, and lessons it reveals.

As you look at your calendar below, note any key dates, intentions, or aligned actions connected to your card's energy. Keep the card nearby as a reminder of your focus and inspiration throughout the month.

CARD OF THE MONTH:

HIGHLIGHTS:

SUN	MON	TUE	WED	THU	FRI	SAT

Monthly Tarot Card (November)

TAROT CARD:

ENERGY & THEMES FOR THE MONTH
What energy is this card inviting you to embody? What opportunities or challenges might arise?

INTENTIONS & ALIGNED ACTIONS
What do you want to create, experience, or shift this month? Translate your insights into clear intentions and aligned actions.

SIGNS & SYNCHRONICITIES
As the month unfolds, note any patterns, symbols, or moments that mirror your card's message.

END-OF-MONTH REFLECTION
Return to your card and reflect: What unfolded? What did you learn? How did this card support your growth?

NOV 01
CARD OF THE DAY:
▷ INTENTION
▷ REFLECTION

NOV 02
CARD OF THE DAY:
▷ INTENTION
▷ REFLECTION

NOV 03
CARD OF THE DAY:
▷ INTENTION
▷ REFLECTION

NOV 04
CARD OF THE DAY:
▷ INTENTION
▷ REFLECTION

NOV 05
CARD OF THE DAY:
▷ INTENTION
▷ REFLECTION

NOV 06
CARD OF THE DAY:
▷ INTENTION
▷ REFLECTION

NOV 07
CARD OF THE DAY:
▷ INTENTION
▷ REFLECTION

NOV 08
CARD OF THE DAY:
▷ INTENTION
▷ REFLECTION

NOV 09
CARD OF THE DAY:
▷ INTENTION
▷ REFLECTION

NOV 10
CARD OF THE DAY:
▷ INTENTION
▷ REFLECTION

NOV 11
CARD OF THE DAY:
▷ INTENTION
▷ REFLECTION

NOV 12
CARD OF THE DAY:
▷ INTENTION
▷ REFLECTION

NOV 13
CARD OF THE DAY:
▷ INTENTION
▷ REFLECTION

NOV 14
CARD OF THE DAY:
▷ INTENTION
▷ REFLECTION

NOV 15
CARD OF THE DAY:
▷ INTENTION
▷ REFLECTION

NOV 16
CARD OF THE DAY:
▷ INTENTION
▷ REFLECTION

NOV 17
CARD OF THE DAY:
▷ INTENTION
▷ REFLECTION

NOV 18
CARD OF THE DAY:
▷ INTENTION
▷ REFLECTION

NOV 19
CARD OF THE DAY:
▷ INTENTION
▷ REFLECTION

NOV 20
CARD OF THE DAY:
▷ INTENTION
▷ REFLECTION

NOV 21
CARD OF THE DAY:
▷ INTENTION
▷ REFLECTION

NOV 22
CARD OF THE DAY:
▷ INTENTION
▷ REFLECTION

NOV 23
CARD OF THE DAY:
▷ INTENTION
▷ REFLECTION

NOV 24
CARD OF THE DAY:
▷ INTENTION
▷ REFLECTION

NOV 25
CARD OF THE DAY:
▷ INTENTION
▷ REFLECTION

NOV 26
CARD OF THE DAY:
▷ INTENTION
▷ REFLECTION

NOV 27
CARD OF THE DAY:
▷ INTENTION
▷ REFLECTION

NOV 28
CARD OF THE DAY:
▷ INTENTION
▷ REFLECTION

NOV 29   CARD OF THE DAY:
▷ INTENTION   ▷ REFLECTION

NOV 30   CARD OF THE DAY:
▷ INTENTION   ▷ REFLECTION

END OF MONTH INSIGHTS

DECEMBER

Monthly Ritual

Start this month by pulling a Tarot card and asking, "What energy am I calling in this month?" Reflect on its message—the opportunities, challenges, and lessons it reveals.

As you look at your calendar below, note any key dates, intentions, or aligned actions connected to your card's energy. Keep the card nearby as a reminder of your focus and inspiration throughout the month.

CARD OF THE MONTH:

HIGHLIGHTS:

SUN	MON	TUE	WED	THU	FRI	SAT

Monthly Tarot Card (December)

TAROT CARD:

ENERGY & THEMES FOR THE MONTH
What energy is this card inviting you to embody? What opportunities or challenges might arise?

INTENTIONS & ALIGNED ACTIONS
What do you want to create, experience, or shift this month? Translate your insights into clear intentions and aligned actions.

SIGNS & SYNCHRONICITIES
As the month unfolds, note any patterns, symbols, or moments that mirror your card's message.

END-OF-MONTH REFLECTION
Return to your card and reflect: What unfolded? What did you learn? How did this card support your growth?

DEC 01
▷ INTENTION　　　　　　　　　　　　CARD OF THE DAY:
▷ REFLECTION

DEC 02
▷ INTENTION　　　　　　　　　　　　CARD OF THE DAY:
▷ REFLECTION

DEC 03
▷ INTENTION　　　　　　　　　　　　CARD OF THE DAY:
▷ REFLECTION

DEC 04
▷ INTENTION　　　　　　　　　　　　CARD OF THE DAY:
▷ REFLECTION

DEC 05
▷ INTENTION　　　　　　　　　　　　CARD OF THE DAY:
▷ REFLECTION

DEC 06
▷ INTENTION　　　　　　　　　　　　CARD OF THE DAY:
▷ REFLECTION

DEC 07
▷ INTENTION　　　　　　　　　　　　CARD OF THE DAY:
▷ REFLECTION

DEC 08
▷ INTENTION   ▷ REFLECTION
CARD OF THE DAY:

DEC 09
▷ INTENTION   ▷ REFLECTION
CARD OF THE DAY:

DEC 10
▷ INTENTION   ▷ REFLECTION
CARD OF THE DAY:

DEC 11
▷ INTENTION   ▷ REFLECTION
CARD OF THE DAY:

DEC 12
▷ INTENTION   ▷ REFLECTION
CARD OF THE DAY:

DEC 13
▷ INTENTION   ▷ REFLECTION
CARD OF THE DAY:

DEC 14
▷ INTENTION   ▷ REFLECTION
CARD OF THE DAY:

DEC 15
CARD OF THE DAY:
▷ INTENTION
▷ REFLECTION

DEC 16
CARD OF THE DAY:
▷ INTENTION
▷ REFLECTION

DEC 17
CARD OF THE DAY:
▷ INTENTION
▷ REFLECTION

DEC 18
CARD OF THE DAY:
▷ INTENTION
▷ REFLECTION

DEC 19
CARD OF THE DAY:
▷ INTENTION
▷ REFLECTION

DEC 20
CARD OF THE DAY:
▷ INTENTION
▷ REFLECTION

DEC 21
CARD OF THE DAY:
▷ INTENTION
▷ REFLECTION

DEC 22
▷ INTENTION   ▷ REFLECTION
CARD OF THE DAY:

DEC 23
▷ INTENTION   ▷ REFLECTION
CARD OF THE DAY:

DEC 24
▷ INTENTION   ▷ REFLECTION
CARD OF THE DAY:

DEC 25
▷ INTENTION   ▷ REFLECTION
CARD OF THE DAY:

DEC 26
▷ INTENTION   ▷ REFLECTION
CARD OF THE DAY:

DEC 27
▷ INTENTION   ▷ REFLECTION
CARD OF THE DAY:

DEC 28
▷ INTENTION   ▷ REFLECTION
CARD OF THE DAY:

DEC 29
CARD OF THE DAY:
▷ INTENTION
▷ REFLECTION

DEC 30
CARD OF THE DAY:
▷ INTENTION
▷ REFLECTION

DEC 31
CARD OF THE DAY:
▷ INTENTION
▷ REFLECTION

END OF MONTH INSIGHTS

YEARLY REFLECTION

A thoughtful end-of-year ritual and Tarot spread to help you reflect on the past year's experiences and uncover meaningful insights.

YEARLY REFLECTION

As you come to the end of the year, take some time to reflect on the past 12 months and prepare yourself for the year to come.

For each question, journal your intuitive thoughts first. Then, if you feel called to do so, draw a Tarot card to help you go deeper.

1. What were my biggest achievements this past year?
2. What were my biggest challenges this past year?
3. How have I developed as a person?
4. What did I learn this year?
5. How would I describe the past year in just three words?
6. What aspects of this year can I leave behind?
7. What aspects of this year can I bring with me into the next?
8. What new seeds and opportunities are being planted?

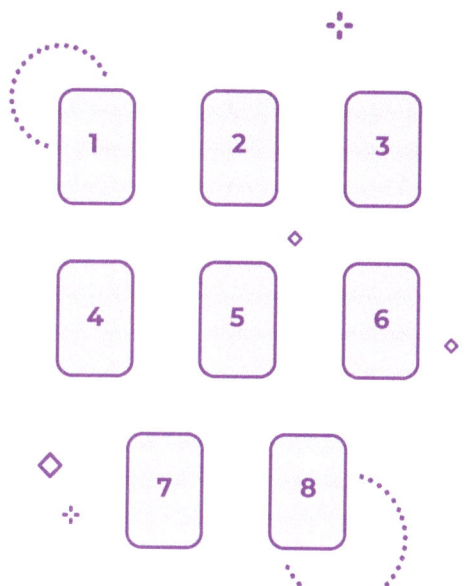

1. WHAT WERE MY BIGGEST ACHIEVEMENTS THIS PAST YEAR?

Don't forget to snap a pic of your reading and share on IG using the hashtag **#biddytarotplanner**. We love seeing you using your Biddy Tarot Planner in action and can't wait to celebrate with you!

2. WHAT WERE MY BIGGEST CHALLENGES FOR THE PAST YEAR?

3. HOW HAVE I DEVELOPED AS A PERSON?

4. WHAT DID I LEARN THIS YEAR?

5. HOW WOULD I DESCRIBE THE PAST YEAR IN JUST THREE WORDS?

6. WHAT ASPECTS OF THIS PAST YEAR CAN I LEAVE BEHIND?

7. WHAT ASPECTS OF THIS PAST YEAR CAN I BRING WITH ME INTO THE NEW YEAR?

8. WHAT NEW SEEDS AND OPPORTUNITIES ARE BEING PLANTED?

SEASONAL SPREADS

Deepen your connection to nature's cycles with reflective Tarot spreads for each equinox and solstice.

SPRING EQUINOX SPREAD

The Spring Equinox honors new growth and opportunity. The seeds that have been planted and nurtured by the rain are now emerging from the earth into the brightness of the sunlight, blossoming into beautiful flowers, fruit, and foliage.

Springtime is filled with colors, scents, and feelings of excitement and anticipation of what's to come. It's the perfect time to explore new possibilities, start new projects, and truly bloom under the rays of this positive light.

Use the following Tarot spread around the time of the Spring Equinox to connect with this sacred energy.

1. What has emerged for me over the Winter period?
2. What lessons have I learned?
3. What new seeds are beginning to sprout?
4. How can I nurture these new opportunities?
5. How am I truly blossoming?
6. How can I best embrace the Spring energy?

INSIGHTS

INSIGHTS

SPRING EQUINOX INTENTIONS

Holding the energy and insight of your Spring Equinox Tarot Reading, set your intentions for the next three months:

SUMMER SOLSTICE SPREAD

The Summer Solstice is the time to shine and be seen! Watch as your projects crest toward completion, and you feel a burst of energy to take action on the new opportunities that arose during the Springtime.

Use the following Tarot spread around the time of the Summer Solstice to connect with this sacred energy.

1. What new opportunities have emerged over the Spring?
2. How can I bring my current projects to fruition?
3. What is expanding in my life right now?
4. What blessings am I receiving?
5. What truly fulfills me?
6. How can I shine my light in the world?

INSIGHTS

INSIGHTS

SUMMER SOLSTICE INTENTIONS

Holding the energy and insight of your Summer Solstice Tarot Reading, set your intentions for the next three months:

FALL EQUINOX SPREAD

The Fall Equinox is the time of harvest. After the abundance of summer, it's time to reap what you've sown, celebrate with deep appreciation, then bunker down for the winter season.

This is the perfect time to slow down, express gratitude for what you've achieved, and gather your resources for the winter period. Use the following Tarot spread around the Fall Equinox to connect with this sacred energy.

1. What have I achieved during the Summer period?
2. What gifts has my harvest given me?
3. What am I truly grateful for?
4. What resources are available to me now?
5. What resources do I need to gather?
6. What can I release and let go?

INSIGHTS

INSIGHTS

FALL EQUINOX INTENTIONS

Holding the energy and insight of your Fall Equinox Tarot Reading, set your intentions for the next three months:

WINTER SOLSTICE SPREAD

The Winter Solstice is the perfect time to go within and hibernate. It's time to reflect on your shadow self — the part of you that you try to deny or hide from others.

Through this self-reflection, you'll emerge once again into the light as your most powerful self. Use the following Tarot spread during the Winter Solstice to connect with this sacred energy.

1. What is the essence of my inner shadow self?
2. What can I learn from my shadow self?
3. How can I bring my shadow self into the light?
4. What lights me up from within?
5. What new seeds am I planting?
6. What do I need to release in order to create space for growth?

INSIGHTS

INSIGHTS

WINTER SOLSTICE INTENTIONS

Holding the energy and insight of your Winter Solstice Tarot Reading, set your intentions for the next three months:

LUNAR SPREADS

Harness the energy of the lunar cycles with Tarot spreads tailored to every zodiac sign, helping you align with cosmic shifts.

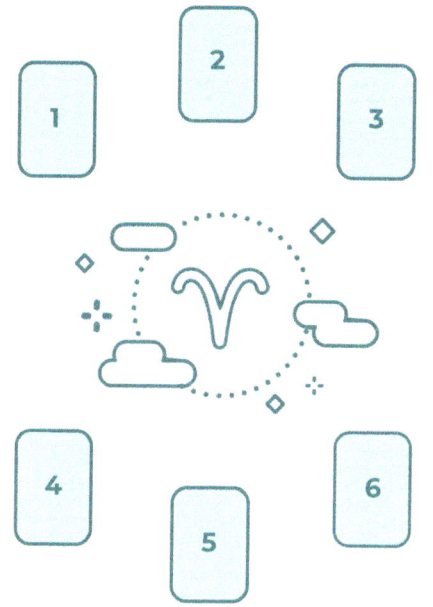

NEW MOON IN ARIES

Use the extra dose of Aries courage to set bold intentions at this New Moon. What risks would you take if you knew you would succeed?

1. What steps should I take to align with my true desires?
2. Where can I channel my passion to reap rewards in the next six months?
3. What can I become more excited about?
4. How could I be more compassionate toward others?
5. What can I do to boost my self-confidence?
6. How can I handle conflict more effectively?

INSIGHTS

On Instagram? Post a photo of your spread and your Tarot Planner with the hashtag #biddytarotplanner and we'll share with the Biddy Tarot community!

FULL MOON IN ARIES

Honor your inner warrior with the Full Moon in Aries. Celebrate the ways you've grown into your strength, and release the fears that hold you back.

1. Where would I benefit most from being more fearless?

2. How can I release stress in a more constructive way?

3. Which battle do I need to let go of?

4. Where do I need to be a little more selfish?

5. What do I need to release to be able to feel strong?

6. How can I be more compassionate toward others?

INSIGHTS

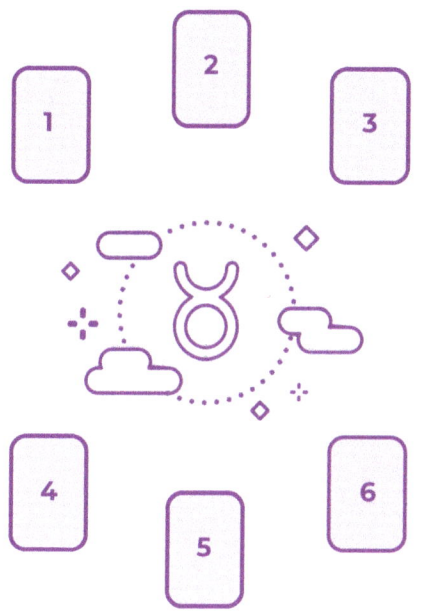

NEW MOON IN TAURUS

With the New Moon in Taurus, you have the chance to consciously create peaceful and pleasurable experiences in your life. Use this energy to develop empowering new habits.

1. What can I do to inspire tranquility in my home?
2. What lessons can I learn from nature?
3. How can I release unhealthy attachments to physical possessions?
4. What simple pleasures would I most enjoy right now?
5. What activities will help me become more grounded in my physical self?
6. What can I do to manage overindulgence?

INSIGHTS

FULL MOON IN TAURUS

The Taurus Full Moon brings the focus to your physical resources and sense of peace. Luxuriate in sensual pleasures and release anything that feels like drama.

1. Which resources that I've gathered in the past 6 months will bring me the most joy?
2. What can I do to inspire more serenity in my life?
3. What do I need to do to feel more physically grounded?
4. How can I achieve a sense of absolute presence in my relationships?
5. What can I let go of now to make life feel easy?
6. How might my relationships benefit from better understanding my sensuality?

INSIGHTS

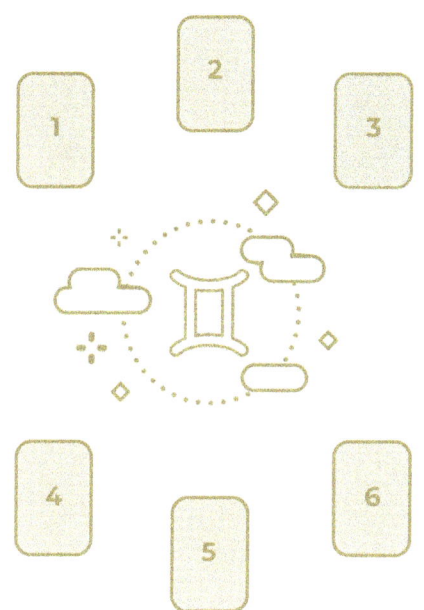

NEW MOON IN GEMINI

A fresh New Moon in Gemini brings a sense of lightness. Set intentions around what you want to learn and teach, and how to best communicate.

1. How can I enhance my perceptions of the world?
2. What am I most curious about right now?
3. Where do I need to learn to verbalize my emotions?
4. What do I have to teach others?
5. What lessons can I learn from others?
6. How can I communicate in new and innovative ways?

INSIGHTS

We love seeing you use your Biddy Tarot Planner! Completed this spread? Make sure you post a pic on Instagram and be sure to use the hashtag **#biddytarotplanner** so we can celebrate with you!

FULL MOON IN GEMINI

The Full Moon in Gemini brings to light the ways you perceive the world. Release any feelings of boredom and explore your curiosities.

1. How have my perceptions of the world changed in the last six months?

2. What new information have I learned that I can teach others?

3. How has verbalizing my emotions impacted my closest relationships this year?

4. What valuable lessons have I learned from others?

5. What valuable lessons have I been able to teach others?

6. How can I approach problems in a more logical and calculated way?

INSIGHTS

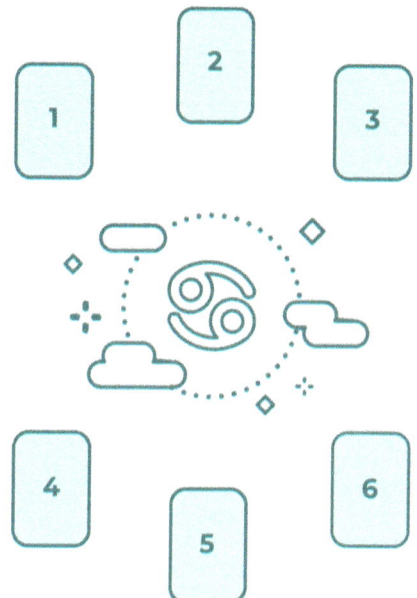

NEW MOON IN CANCER

The New Moon in Cancer is a prime opportunity to make conscious choices about your everyday experiences. Dive into your emotions and set empowering intentions around how you want to feel.

1. What new feelings are coming up for me right now?
2. Where can I be more vulnerable in my relationships?
3. How might I benefit from setting boundaries?
4. How can I level-up my self-care practice?
5. What do I need to know about creating sacred space in my home?
6. What new approach can I take to support my emotional well-being?

INSIGHTS

FULL MOON IN CANCER

Under this nurturing moon, you may find that unresolved emotions or intentions to release the past come to light in a cleansing wave. Embrace this moment as an opportunity for emotional healing and renewal.

1. How have I nurtured my emotional self in the last 6 months?

2. Where in my life am I ready to heal?

3. How can I open my heart whilst maintaining healthy boundaries?

4. Which of my emotions are no longer serving my highest good?

5. Which aspects of myself need mothering now?

6. What do I need to release in order to trust life?

INSIGHTS

NEW MOON IN LEO

Your passions are coming into focus with the New Moon in Leo. Now is the time to set intentions about how you want to show up in the world.

1. What do I most want to create?
2. What can I do to express myself authentically in empowered ways?
3. What new aspects of myself am I discovering?
4. How can I be an effective, compassionate leader?
5. Where am I best placed to lead by example?
6. Which areas of my life may require a little more courage in the next six months?

INSIGHTS

On Instagram? Post a photo of your spread and your Tarot Planner with the hashtag #biddytarotplanner and we'll share with the Biddy Tarot community!

FULL MOON IN LEO

Feel into the fullness of creativity and play, and get ready to shine with the Leo Full Moon. Celebrate your unique warmth and brilliance bathed in this wonderful energy.

1. What am I most proud of achieving in the last six months?

2. How has my past courage impacted my personal growth?

3. What are some limiting beliefs I hold about myself?

4. What new stories can I tell myself instead?

5. Where in my life might I need to be more humble?

6. How could I express myself more authentically this year?

INSIGHTS

NEW MOON IN VIRGO

The New Moon in Virgo is an opportunity to get clear on how you want to serve the world. How can you be your best self during this cycle?

1. How can I be of highest service to the people in my life?
2. Which area of my life would benefit most from a fresh routine?
3. What change might I make to support my physical well-being?
4. What action can I take to bring a sense of order to my environment?
5. What action can I take to process my thoughts more effectively?
6. What action can I take to gain further emotional clarity?

INSIGHTS

FULL MOON IN VIRGO

The Virgo Full Moon invites you to honor the ways you are serving the world and the places you are creating order from chaos.

1. What can I offer to my family and friends to be of the highest service?
2. Which areas of my life might benefit from creating order?
3. How might I benefit from working hard in the next six months?
4. How can I limit clutter in my physical space?
5. What can I do to support my mental clarity?
6. How can I best support healthy emotional expression?

INSIGHTS

Don't forget to snap a pic of your reading and share on IG using the hashtag #biddytarotplanner. We love seeing you using your Biddy Tarot Planner in action and can't wait to celebrate with you!

NEW MOON IN LIBRA

The New Moon in Libra is a beautiful time to explore your personal values, the environment, and the relationships that help you feel balanced.

1. Where in my life would I benefit most from a deeper sense of harmony?
2. How might evaluating my personal style positively affect my life?
3. How can I create more beauty in my environment?
4. Where would I benefit from a more peaceful approach?
5. How can I bond more strongly with others?
6. What is my true intention in my current or future relationship?

INSIGHTS

On Instagram? Post a photo of your spread and your Tarot Planner with the hashtag **#biddytarotplanner** and we'll share with the Biddy Tarot community!

FULL MOON IN LIBRA

The Libra Full Moon invites you to revel in beauty and release anything that negatively impacts your sense of harmony and balance.

1. What support might help me make the best choices?

2. What can I do to create more balance in my relationships?

3. Where is the greatest imbalance in my life right now?

4. What do I need to release to be more objective moving forward?

5. What do I need to do to feel more confident in my decisions?

6. How can I manifest more beauty in my life?

INSIGHTS

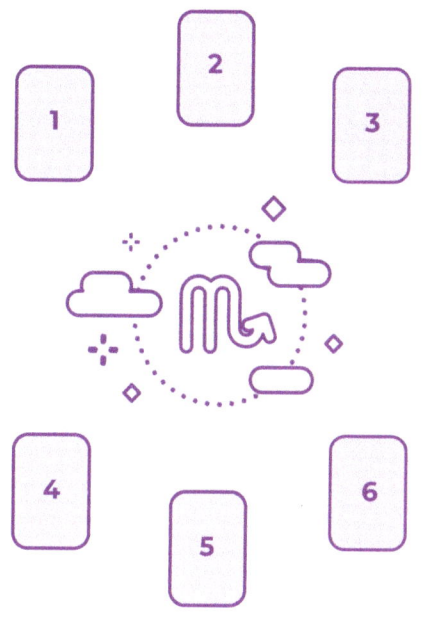

NEW MOON IN SCORPIO

The New Moon in Scorpio is a time to make conscious decisions about your spiritual transformation. Set your intentions about who you're becoming and where you'd like to go.

1. Which area of my life might experience the deepest transformation in the next six months?
2. How can I healthily express my deepest desires?
3. Which elements of my shadow self need some attention and care?
4. How can I release the desire to control or manipulate outcomes?
5. Where am I not being truly honest with myself?
6. How can I foster a deeper connection with my spiritual truth?

INSIGHTS

FULL MOON IN SCORPIO

The intense Scorpio Full Moon sets the stage for shadow work and transformational activities. Use this energy to release anything that no longer serves you.

1. What feelings have I been avoiding?

2. What lessons has pain taught me over the past six months?

3. What intense emotions are coming up for me now?

4. How can I express my emotions in a healthier way?

5. What do I need to release to experience deep transformation?

6. Where do I need to relinquish control in my life?

INSIGHTS

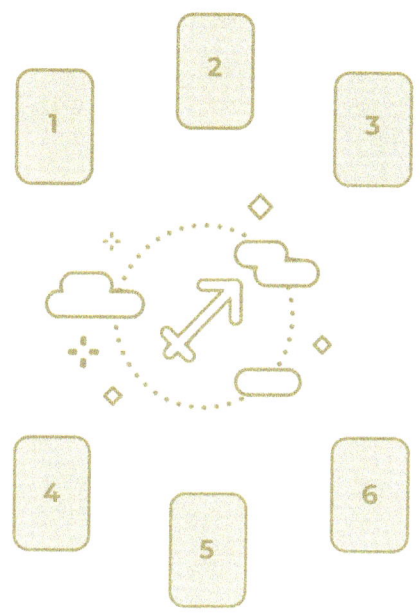

NEW MOON IN SAGITTARIUS

The New Moon in Sagittarius encourages you to expand your awareness and perspective. Set intentions around adventures and experiences that will broaden your worldview.

1. Where do I need to focus on expanding my awareness?
2. What can I do to inspire a sense of adventure in my life?
3. What can I do to expand my friendship circles and connect with new people?
4. What is my ideal vision for the global community?
5. What lessons have I learned from short or long-term travel in the past 6 months?
6. How can I utilize those lessons to inspire others?

INSIGHTS

We love seeing you use your Biddy Tarot Planner! Completed this spread? Make sure you post a pic on Instagram and be sure to use the hashtag **#biddytarotplanner** so we can celebrate with you!

FULL MOON IN SAGITTARIUS

You can expect heightened ideas and visions during this Full Moon in Sagittarius. Tap into this expansive energy and release anything that's keeping you small.

1. Where do I need to focus on expanding my awareness?
2. What do I need to release in order to achieve my goals?
3. What is my ideal vision for the global community?
4. How might short or long-term travel benefit me in the next six months?
5. What can I do to connect more deeply with my friends?
6. What is my guiding vision for the future?

INSIGHTS

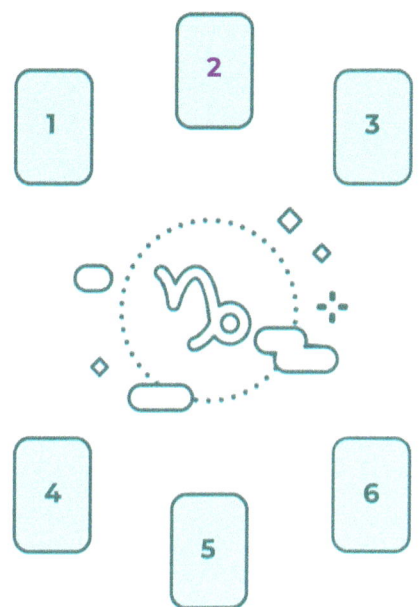

NEW MOON IN CAPRICORN

Since Capricorn rules stability, structure, and goals, this New Moon is a great time to work on a solid plan that will bring your dreams to life in the new year.

1. What insights did I gain this year around what I want to achieve next year?
2. Which areas of my life might benefit from creating a sense of order?
3. How can I best support my financial goals this year?
4. What goals do I want to achieve within the next six months?
5. What kind of structure do I need to establish to support those goals?
6. Which grounding practices would best support me this year?

INSIGHTS

We love seeing you use your Biddy Tarot Planner! Completed this spread? Make sure you post a pic on Instagram and be sure to use the hashtag #biddytarotplanner so we can celebrate with you!

FULL MOON IN CAPRICORN

The Full Moon in Capricorn is a powerful time to reflect on your achievements. Where have you stood in integrity and built something you're proud of?

1. What am I most proud of achieving in the past six months?
2. What foundations do I most need to establish now to support future success?
3. What is a non-negotiable for me right now?
4. How can I help motivate others to work toward their own goals?
5. Which limiting beliefs are preventing me from setting bigger goals?
6. Where do I need to make more ethical choices?

INSIGHTS

NEW MOON IN AQUARIUS

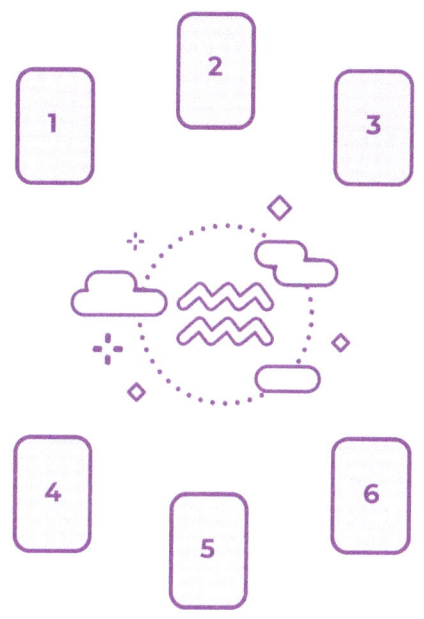

The Aquarius New Moon is an opportunity to set out-of-the-box intentions. Let go of what others think and make your plans according to what you want.

1. What unique gifts do I bring to the table?

2. How can I best use these gifts to uplift humanity?

3. Where would I most like to see social change and equality?

4. How am I best placed to communicate my ideas with the world?

5. How can I connect with others who align with my future vision?

6. Which areas of my life would benefit from expressing vulnerability?

INSIGHTS

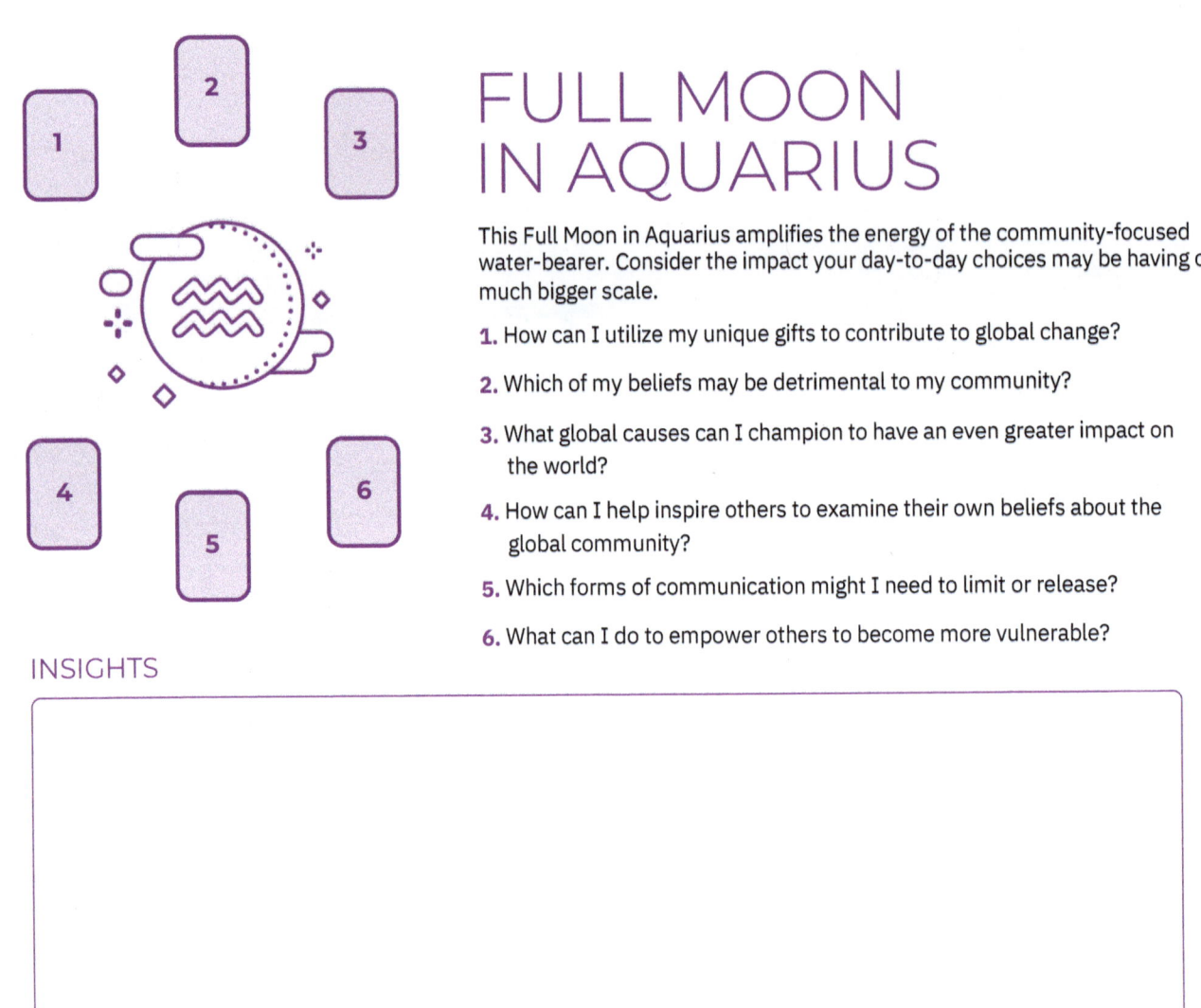

FULL MOON IN AQUARIUS

This Full Moon in Aquarius amplifies the energy of the community-focused water-bearer. Consider the impact your day-to-day choices may be having on a much bigger scale.

1. How can I utilize my unique gifts to contribute to global change?
2. Which of my beliefs may be detrimental to my community?
3. What global causes can I champion to have an even greater impact on the world?
4. How can I help inspire others to examine their own beliefs about the global community?
5. Which forms of communication might I need to limit or release?
6. What can I do to empower others to become more vulnerable?

INSIGHTS

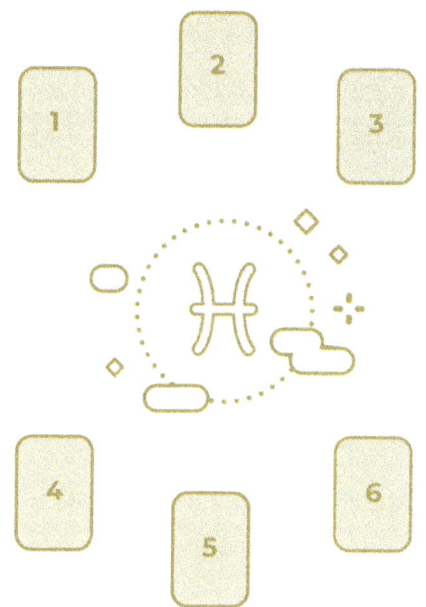

NEW MOON IN PISCES

This Pisces New Moon, let your imagination run wild and dream big. Set intentions to bring your intuitive vision to life.

1. How can I connect more deeply with my intuition?
2. What can I do to bring myself into alignment with the highest good?
3. What am I currently manifesting in my life?
4. How can I align my emotions to support positive manifestations?
5. What new creative projects am I called to begin now?
6. How can I further develop my spiritual practice?

INSIGHTS

We love seeing you use your Biddy Tarot Planner! Completed this spread? Make sure you post a pic on Instagram and be sure to use the hashtag **#biddytarotplanner** so we can celebrate with you!

FULL MOON IN PISCES

A dreamy Full Moon in Pisces can intensify your connection to your intuition. Celebrate your manifestations and release anything that isn't serving you.

1. Which areas of my life have benefited most from my intuition?
2. What do I need to release to connect more deeply with myself?
3. Where do I need to focus more on gratitude in the next six months?
4. What limiting beliefs must I release to expand my creative projects?
5. What can I focus on to deepen my spiritual practice?
6. How might the arts inspire my creative success?

INSIGHTS

LEARN TO READ TAROT INTUITIVELY...

Access these Biddy Tarot learning resources to activate your intuition and reach YOUR highest potential. Learn more about these resources — and our full range of Tarot courses and programs — to help you on your journey at www.biddytarot.com/shop.

THE BIDDY TAROT DECK
Elevate Your Tarot Experience Today!

Whether you're a seasoned Tarot reader or just beginning your journey, the Biddy Tarot Deck is a powerful companion that will accompany you on your path of self-discovery and personal growth. Don't miss the opportunity to add this exquisite deck to your collection. The purple gilded edge and hand-drawn imagery add an exquisite touch of elegance, making this deck an irresistible treasure for Tarot enthusiasts and collectors alike. Experience the magic, wisdom, and beauty of Tarot in a whole new light with the Biddy Tarot Deck. Tap into your inner wisdom and unlock the secrets of the Universe.

Get your hands on this delightful deck now! Available for purchase at www.biddytarot.com/deck.

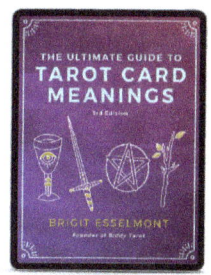

THE ULTIMATE GUIDE TO TAROT CARD MEANINGS
Fresh, Modern, Practical Guide To The Meanings Of Every Tarot Card

The *Ultimate Guide to Tarot Card Meanings* has everything you need to read the Tarot cards as simply as reading a magazine. Just imagine — all the Tarot card meanings you could ever want, right at your fingertips in this comprehensive, 400+ page reference guide. You'll never need to buy another book on Tarot card meanings again!

Available for purchase at www.biddytarot.com/guide.

MASTER THE TAROT CARD MEANINGS PROGRAM
Stop Memorizing the Cards and Start Listening to Your Intuition

The *Master the Tarot Card meanings* program will help you learn to read Tarot intuitively. Each lesson empowers you to build a unique personal connection with the Tarot, using simple yet powerful techniques for interpreting the cards. In just seven modules, you'll unlock the secrets of the Major and Minor Arcana, Court Cards, and reversed readings using Numerology, Symbolism, and so much more. By the end of the program, you'll have the power to intuitively access the meaning behind any spread!

Available for purchase at www.biddytarot.com/mtcm.

THE COLLECTIVE
Grow faster, go deeper, and transform your life from the inside out – with the mentorship, structure and support of a global community

The Biddy Tarot Collective is the only online community of its kind. Connect with Tarot lovers all over the world and get resources to help you learn and grow in your practice. Members access an expansive library of Tarot resources, the Practice Reading Exchange, Monthly Energy Forecasts with Brigit, and a Moon Manifesting Ceremonies to help you level up on your Tarot journey.

Join the Biddy Tarot Community at www.biddytarot.com/thecollective.

www.ingramcontent.com/pod-product-compliance
Lightning Source LLC
Chambersburg PA
CBHW061807290426
44109CB00031B/2954